PowerKids Readers:

Big Cats
CHEETAHS

Elizabeth Vogel

The Rosen Publishing Group's
PowerKids Press™
New York

1

Published in 2002 by The Rosen Publishing Group, Inc.
29 East 21st Street, New York, NY 10010

First Edition

Book design: Michael Donnellan

Photo Credits: p. 1 © Ronn Maratea/International Stock; pp. 5, 7, 9, and 13 © Digital Vision Ltd.; p. 11 © J & B Photographers/Animals Animals; p. 15 © Norbert Rosing/Animals Animals; pp. 17, 19 © A. & M. Shah/Animals Animals; p. 21 © Tony Miller/FPG International.

Vogel, Elizabeth.
Cheetahs / Elizabeth Vogel.— 1st ed.
        p. cm. — (Big cats)
Includes bibliographical references (p.   ).
ISBN 0-8239-6023-4 (lib. bdg.)
1. Cheetah—Juvenile literature. [1. Cheetah.] I. Title.
QL737.C23 V63 2002
599.75'9—dc21

                                                                    00-013014

Manufactured in the United States of America

CONTENTS

Cheetahs are big cats
who live in the wild.

5

Cheetahs have beautiful fur. They have yellow fur with black spots.

Cheetahs have two black stripes running from their eyes to their mouths. These stripes are called tear marks.

9

Cheetahs love to run.
Cheetahs are the fastest
animals in the world.

Cheetahs do not growl or roar. They hiss, or chirp like birds do.

Cheetahs like to eat meat. Sometimes they eat gazelles.

Baby cheetahs are called kittens. They are born in a group called a litter.

When a cheetah litter is born, the kittens are covered in soft, gray fur.

When they are old enough, cheetah kittens learn how to hunt from their mother.

WORDS TO KNOW

gazelle

kittens

litter

tear marks

22

Here are more books to read about cheetahs:
Cheetah
By Taylor Morrison
Henry Holt & Company

Cheetahs
by Don Middleton
Rosen Publishing

To learn more about cheetahs, check out these Web sites:
www.cheetah.org/home.htm
www.cheetahspot.com
www.pbs.org/wnet/nature/cheetahs/

INDEX

Word Count: 114

Note to Librarians, Teachers, and Parents

PowerKids Readers are specially designed to help emergent and beginning readers build their skills in reading for information. Simple vocabulary and concepts are paired with stunning, detailed images from the natural world around them. Readers will respond to written language by linking meaning with their own everyday experiences and observations. Sentences are short and simple, employing a basic vocabulary of sight words, as well as new words that describe objects or processes that take place in the natural world. Large type, clean design, and photographs corresponding directly to the text all help children to decipher meaning. Features such as a contents page, picture glossary, and index help children to get the most out of PowerKids Readers. They also introduce children to the basic elements of a book, which they will encounter in their future reading experiences. Lists of related books and Web sites encourage kids to explore other sources and to continue the process of learning.